Space

Words by James A. Seevers
Associate Astronomer
The Adler Planetarium

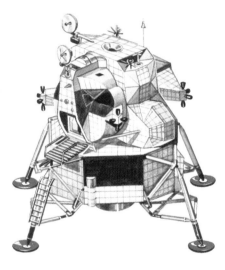

Raintree Childrens Books
Milwaukee

Cover Photo: NASA.

Library of Congress Number: 87-20801
1 2 3 4 5 6 7 8 9   92 91 90 89 88 87

Printed and bound in the United States of America

Library of Congress Cataloging in Publication Data

Seevers, James A.
  Space.

  Bibliography: p. 47
  Summary: Discusses aspects of space exploration
including the solar system, different spacecrafts,
and the achievements of several astronauts.
    1. Outer space—Exploration—Juvenile literature.
2. Astronautics—Juvenile literature. [1. Outer
space—Exploration. 2. Astronautics] I. Title.
TL793.S36   1987   629.4   87-20801
ISBN 0-8172-3260-5 (lib. bdg.)
ISBN 0-8172-3265-0 (softcover)

Space

The clouds you see in the sky float in the layer of air above the earth. This layer of air is called the atmosphere. The sun is far beyond the atmosphere. It floats in space. There is no air.

At night you can see the stars and the moon in the sky. The twinkling stars look tiny. But they are really big suns. They look tiny because they are so far away. The moon looks much bigger than the stars. That is because it is much closer to the earth.

For many years people only dreamed about going to the moon and the other planets. Now people travel in space, thousands of miles from earth.

The problem in getting into space was the earth's gravity. If you throw a ball into the air, it always comes back down again. The earth's gravity pulls the ball back. The harder you throw it, the faster and higher it goes. If you could make it go fast enough, it would go into space.

There are rockets that go into space. A rocket going 18,000 miles an hour (28,968 kilometers an hour) will go into space and stay there. It circles the earth outside the atmosphere. The path it goes in is called its orbit. To get away from the earth's pull, the rocket must go even faster. It must go 25,000 miles an hour (40,234 kilometers an hour).

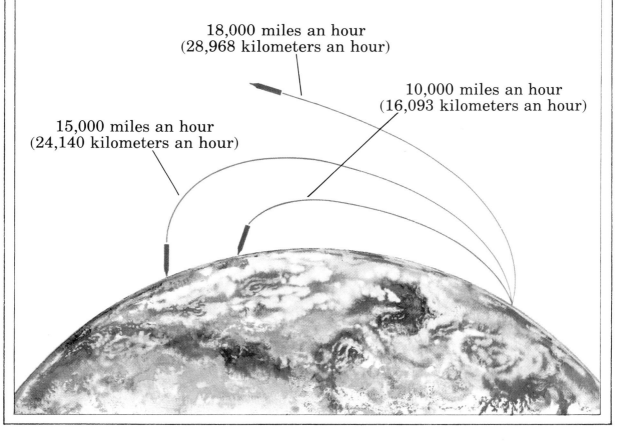

18,000 miles an hour
(28,968 kilometers an hour)

10,000 miles an hour
(16,093 kilometers an hour)

15,000 miles an hour
(24,140 kilometers an hour)

Firework rockets are the simplest kinds of rockets. They work the way that rockets for spacecraft do, but they use gunpowder for fuel. The gunpowder fuel is burned to make hot gases. The hot gases shoot out of the end of the rocket and push it forward.

The giant rockets
that go into space
work much as
firework rockets
do. But they are
much bigger.

This one takes
people to the moon.
It is 364 feet (111
meters) high.

jet of air

How does a rocket work? You can see for yourself. Blow up a balloon and let it go. Just watch it fly.

Why does it fly? The balloon pushes the air out. As the air rushes out of the balloon, the balloon is pushed forward.

More than one rocket is needed to push the spacecraft into orbit. Often three rockets are put together, one on top of the other. Each one is called a stage. They fall away when their fuel is burned up.

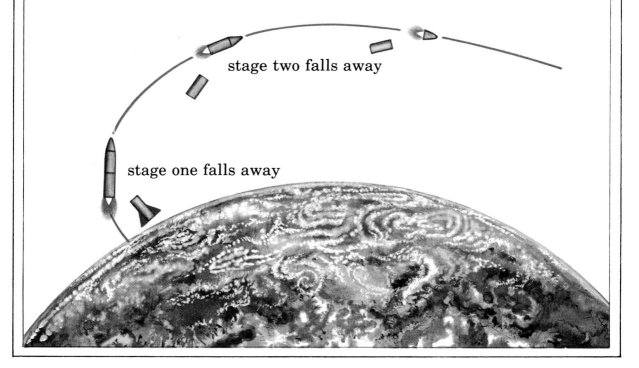

stage two falls away

stage one falls away

Rockets that go into space are over 100 feet (30 meters) tall. They use special kinds of fuels.

This picture shows a rocket taking off. The rocket is being pushed into the air by the hot gases shooting out of the bottom of the rocket.

On top of the rocket is a spacecraft. Soon it will be traveling in space. An object that orbits in space is called a satellite.

How does a satellite stay up in the sky? It is like a stone being spun around on a piece of string. The spinning pushes the stone out. The string stops the stone. It holds it back. The two forces, one pulling and one pushing, make the stone move in a circle.

The earth's gravity works the same way. When a satellite is launched, the rocket pushes it away from the earth. The earth's gravity pulls it back, but it can't stop it completely. These two forces are what make a satellite orbit.

satellite in orbit

Satellites can be used to do many things. Some satellites carry television cameras. They take pictures of clouds in the earth's atmosphere. They are called weather satellites. The cloud pictures help to tell what the weather will be like a few days later. The name of the weather satellite in the picture is Tiros.

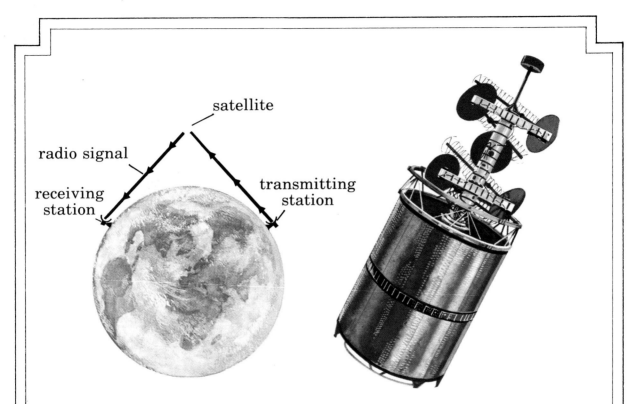

Some satellites send radio and television signals from one country to another. These satellites are called communications satellites. A transmitter can send a signal into space to the satellite. The satellite then sends the signal to a receiving station in another part of the world. Today there are many satellites sending signals all over the world.

Other satellites carry people.
People who travel in space are called
astronauts. The spacecraft that
astronauts travel in are much larger
than ordinary spacecraft. They are
made up of two sections.

The picture shows part of the
Apollo spacecraft. It carried three
astronauts to the moon. They lived in
the top section. It had air for them to
breathe. Above them was a
compartment for a parachute. The
parachute was used for their return to
earth. Only this section came back
to earth.

The other section held all kinds of
equipment. It held batteries, the
rocket, and fuel.

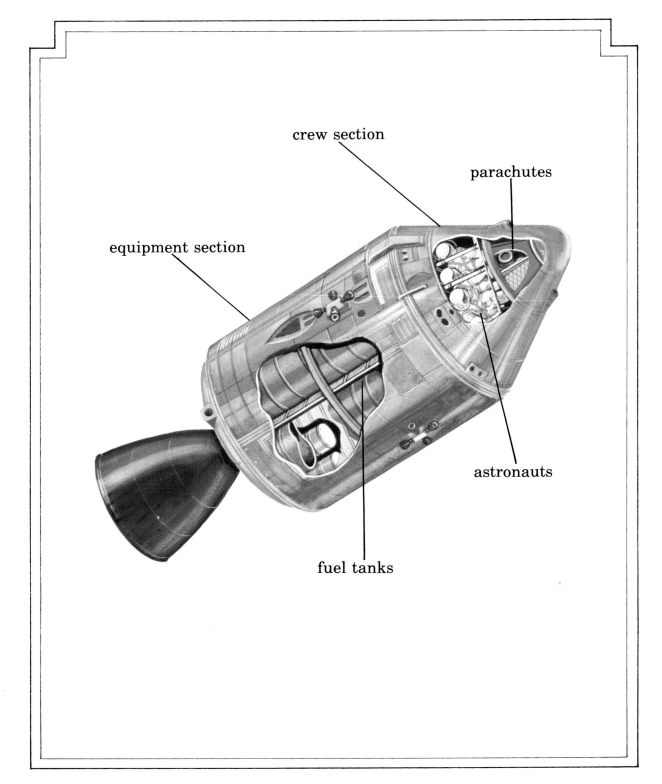

crew section

parachutes

equipment section

astronauts

fuel tanks

Before the Apollo astronauts blasted off, they were over 300 feet (91 meters) in the air. Their spacecraft sat on top of the giant rocket that lifted them into space.

The picture shows the Apollo spacecraft. The crew section is at the top. The crew section is also called the command module. The equipment section is in the middle. At the bottom is another little spacecraft. This is the spacecraft that landed on the moon. It is called a lunar module.

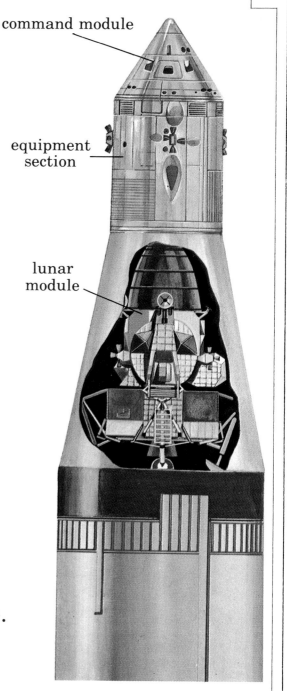

command module

equipment section

lunar module

First the astronauts entered the
spacecraft. Then they strapped themselves
to padded couches. Then the rocket was
started. The rocket pushed very hard and
fast as it lifted them into space. If they had
not been strapped to the couches, they
might have been thrown against something
inside of the spacecraft.

As each rocket stage was fired, they were lifted faster and farther into space. When they got far enough into space, they put the spacecraft in its orbit around the earth. Then they turned the last rocket off.

When they unstrapped themselves, they found out that they were weightless. They floated in midair inside their cabin. Everything in the cabin was weightless. It was difficult to eat and drink. Water would not pour from a glass. The astronauts had to use straws. Their food was made into paste. It was in a tube that looked like a toothpaste tube. The astronauts squeezed the paste into their mouths.

On later spaceflights, astronauts ate regular food. They liked it better, but they still had to be careful when they ate.

There isn't any air in space. The spacecraft has its own supply of air. The astronauts can breathe this air inside the spacecraft. Sometimes they have to go outside the spacecraft. Then they wear a special suit called a space suit.

The space suit has its own air supply. The suit has a number of layers. The top layer is made of a very shiny material. It protects the astronaut's body from the great heat and cold in space. The helmet has special glass. It protects the astronaut's eyes from the strong light of the sun.

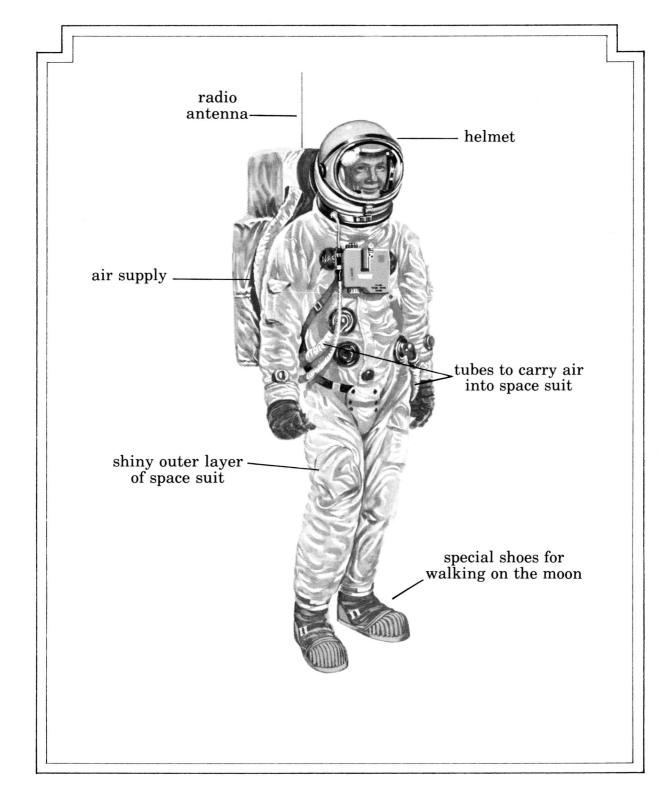

radio antenna —

helmet

air supply —

tubes to carry air into space suit

shiny outer layer of space suit

special shoes for walking on the moon

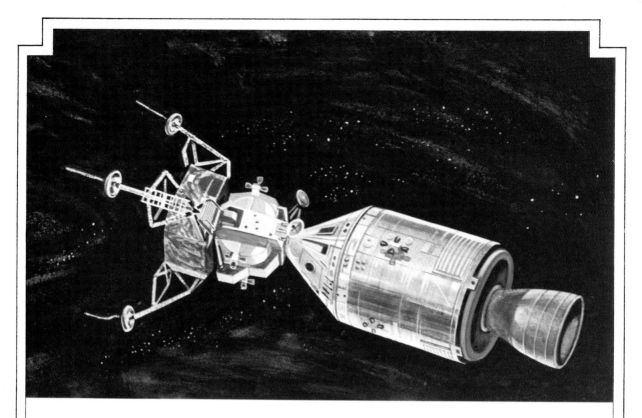

When the astronauts were ready to go
to the moon, they fired the last rocket
stage. It made the spacecraft go even faster.
It went so fast that the earth's gravity no
longer held it back. It shot farther out into
space and was on its way to the moon.
Next, the astronauts used small rockets to
pull the command module away from
the moonship.

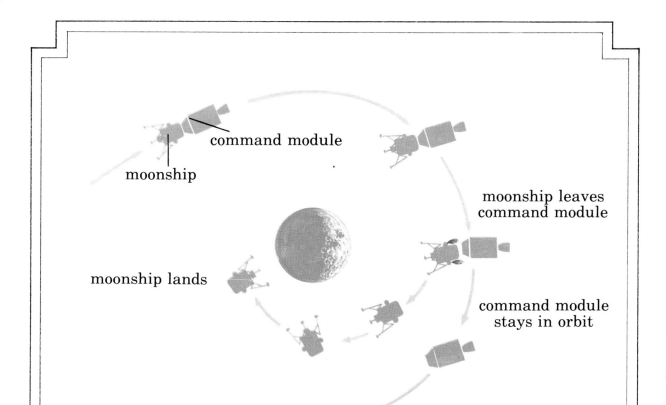

command module

moonship

moonship leaves
command module

moonship lands

command module
stays in orbit

Three days later, the astronauts were
near the moon. They fired a rocket that
pushed backwards. That slowed them down. As
they got closer, they went into orbit around
the moon. Then two astronauts crawled into
the moonship. The moonship has its own
engine. They fired it, and the moonship
slowly dropped to the moon. The command
module stayed in orbit.

After they landed on the moon, the astronauts got ready to go outside and explore. The moon does not have an atmosphere. On the moon, people are not protected from the sun and the heat and cold. This is why astronauts must wear space suits. The space suits give them air to breathe. They also protect them from the sun and the temperature.

Where there is no air, there is no life. The moon is a dead, silent world. All over it are lumps of rocks and great pits called craters. The soil is soft and crumbly. When the astronauts walked on it, they left big footprints.

The moon has gravity, but it is not as strong as the earth's. This made the astronauts feel much lighter than they did on earth.

When it was time to leave, the astronauts climbed back into the moonship. They started the engines and took off. Then they returned to the command module. The command module is the only part that returns to earth.

The Apollo, like all spacecraft, was moving very fast when it entered the earth's atmosphere. The air rubbed against it. This rubbing slowed it down. It also made the spacecraft so hot that it became red.

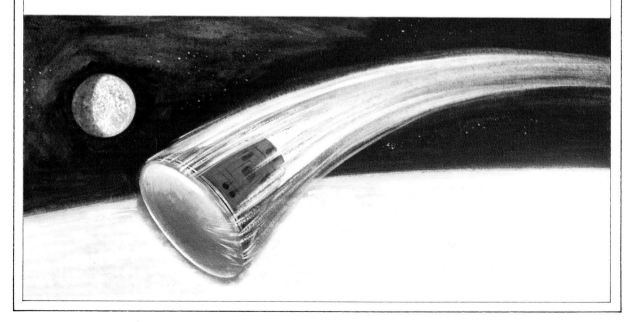

As the spacecraft came closer to earth, the parachutes at the top of the command module opened. They slowed the spacecraft down much more. This was so it could gently land in the ocean. Helicopters from a ship rushed to the landing place and picked up the spacecraft. They carried it back to the ship.

Spacecraft that go far into space are called probes. Probes can take very good pictures of planets.

One probe is the Viking Orbiter. It circled Mars and took many pictures. The Viking Orbiter also had a small landing craft in it. The Viking landing craft landed on Mars. It took many close-up pictures of the surface. The Viking probe showed that there was some air on Mars. The probe also dug up some soil. Tests of the soil showed that there is no life on Mars.

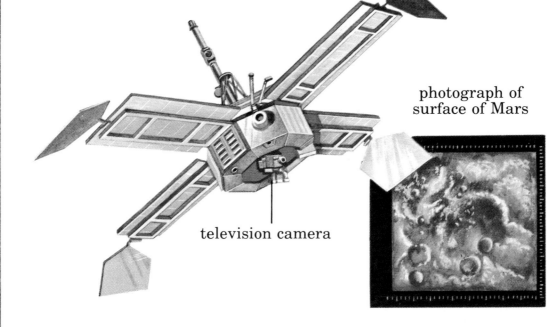

photograph of surface of Mars

television camera

This is a special satellite. It is called a space shuttle. It takes off like a rocket, but it lands like an airplane. The space shuttle has a cargo section. The cargo section can carry instruments. It can also carry small satellites that can be put into orbit from the shuttle.

Someday people may be able to live in large space colonies. The colonies will have their own air, water, and plants. Living in a space colony will be like living on earth.

The Metric System

In the United States, things are measured in inches, pounds, quarts, and so on. That system is called the American system. Most other countries of the world use centimeters, kilograms, and liters to measure those things. That system is called the metric system.

At one time the United States was going to change to the metric system. That is why you will see both systems of measurement in some books. For example, you might see a sentence like this: "That bicycle wheel is 27 inches (69 centimeters) across."

Most books you use will have only one system of measurement. You may want to change from one system to the other. The chart on the next page will help you.

All you have to do is multiply the unit of measurement in Column 1 by the number in Column 2. Your answer will be the unit in Column 3.

Suppose you want to change 15 centimeters to inches. First, find *centimeters* in Column 1. Next, multiply 15 times .4. The answer you get is 6. So, 15 centimeters equal 6 inches.

Column 1	Column 2	Column 3
THIS UNIT OF MEASUREMENT	TIMES THIS NUMBER	GIVES THIS UNIT OF MEASUREMENT
inches	2.54	centimeters
feet	30.	centimeters
feet	.3	meters
yards	.9	meters
miles	1.6	kilometers
ounces	28.	grams
pounds	.45	kilograms
fluid ounces	.03	liters
pints	.47	liters
quarts	.95	liters
gallons	3.8	liters
centimeters	.4	inches
meters	1.1	yards
kilometers	.6	miles
grams	.035	ounces
kilograms	2.2	pounds
liters	33.8	fluid ounces
liters	2.1	pints
liters	1.06	quarts
liters	.26	gallons

Where to Read
About Space

Pronunciation Key

a	a as in **cat, bad**
ā	a as in **able**, ai as in **train**, ay as in **play**
ä	a as in **father, car**, o as in **cot**
e	e as in **bend, yet**
ē	e as in **me**, ee as in **feel**, ea as in **beat**, ie as in **piece**, y as in **heavy**
i	i as in **in, pig**, e as in **pocket**
ī	i as in **ice, time**, ie as in **tie**, y as in **my**
o	o as in **top**, a as in **watch**
ō	o as in **old**, oa as in **goat**, ow as in **slow**, oe as in **toe**
ô	o as in **cloth**, au as in **caught**, aw as in **paw**, a as in **all**
oo	oo as in **good**, u as in **put**
o͞o	oo as in **tool**, ue as in **blue**
oi	oi as in **oil**, oy as in **toy**
ou	ou as in **out**, ow as in **plow**
u	u as in **up, gun**, o as in **other**
ur	ur as in **fur**, er as in **person**, ir as in **bird**, or as in **work**
yo͞o	u as in **use**, ew as in **few**
ə	a as in **again**, e as in **broken**, i as in **pencil**, o as in **attention**, u as in **surprise**
ch	ch as in **such**
ng	ng as in **sing**
sh	sh as in **shell, wish**
th	th as in **three, bath**
t̲h̲	th as in **that, together**

GLOSSARY

These words are defined the way they are used in this book

aluminum (ə lōō′ mə nəm′) a light metal used to build things

astronaut (as′ trə nôt′) a person who travels in space

atmosphere (at′ məs fēr′) the air around the earth

battery (bat′ ər ē) something that can make or store electricity

beyond (bē änd′) farther than; on the other side of

body (bäd′ ē) all of a person from head to foot

breathe (brē<u>th</u>) to take in air with the lungs and force it out again

camera (kam′ ər ə) something for taking pictures or movies

cargo section (kar′ gō sek′ shən) a room or compartment. A space shuttle has a cargo section that can carry instruments and small satellites.

check (chek) to see if something is correct or not broken

clear (klēr) not dark or cloudy

cloud (kloud) a gray or white mass floating in the sky

command module (kə mand′ mäj′ yo͞ol) the part of the spacecraft that stays in orbit around the moon when the lunar module lands on the moon

communications satellite (kə myo͞o′ nə kā′ shənz sat′ ə līt) a satellite that can receive messages from one part of the earth and send them to another part of the earth

compartment (kəm pärt′ mənt) a smaller place separate from the rest of a larger place

complete (kəm plēt′) whole; entire

crater (krā′ tər) one of the great pits on the moon's surface

crew (kro͞o) a group of people working on the same job or project

dead (ded) not alive

difficult (dif′ ə kult) not easy; hard to do

electricity (i lek′ tris′ ə tē) a kind of
energy used to run machines and
heat homes

engine (en′ jin) a machine that is used
to run another machine; a motor

equipment (i kwip′ mənt) tools or
supplies used for a certain purpose

explore (eks plôr′) to travel to a new
place to find out about it

fireworks (fīr′ wərks) firecrackers and
rockets that explode and make loud
noises and sparks

flight (flīt) a trip through the air; flying

float (flōt) to rest in the air or on the
water or to move slowly through the air
or water

footprint (foot′ print) a mark left by
someone walking

force (fôrs) strength or power or pressure

forward (fôr′ wərd) toward the front;
ahead

fuel (fyoo′ əl) something that is burned
to produce heat energy

future (fyo͞o′ chər) a time that has not yet come

gas (gas) something that is not solid or liquid. Air is made up of different gases.

gravity (grav′ ə tē) the force that pulls things toward the center of the earth and gives them weight. The moon and other large heavenly bodies have gravity.

gunpowder (gun′ pou dər) powder that explodes when burned

heat (hēt) high temperature; the state of being hot

helicopter (hel′ ə kop′ tər) an aircraft that flies by means of rotating blades

helmet (hel′ mit) a protective covering for the head

instrument (in′ strə mənt) something used to help do work

iron (ī ərn) a metal used to build things

launch (lônch) to send up into space

layer (lā′ ər) one level or one thickness of something

liquid (lik′ wid) something that is not a solid or a gas. Water is a liquid.

lunar (lo͞o′ nər) having to do with the moon

lunar module (lo͞o′ nər mäj′ yo͞ol) that part of the spacecraft that actually lands on the moon

machine (mə shēn′) something that does work or can be used to do work

material (mə tēr′ ē əl) the thing that something is made of

midair (mid′ ar) in the air or sky

moon (mo͞on) the body that moves around the earth once every 29½ days

moonship (mo͞on′ ship) the part of the spacecraft that actually lands on the moon; lunar module

orbit (ôr′ bit) the path that a planet or satellite travels as it circles a larger body

ordinary (ôrd′ ən er ē) common; usual

pad (pad) to make something softer by adding thick and soft material

parachute (par′ ə sho͞ot) a large object shaped like an umbrella that allows people and things to fall from high places slowly and safely

phone (fōn) a telephone

planet (plan′ it) one of nine heavenly bodies that orbit the sun. The earth is one of the planets.

possible (pos′ ə bəl) is able to happen or be done

probe (prōb) a satellite that can take pictures of other planets

program (prō′ gram) a presentation or performance

proper (prop′ ər) correct

ray (rā) a single beam of light. Sunlight is made of many rays.

receiver (ri sē′ vər) something that changes electrical energy into sounds and pictures

regular (reg′ yə lər) usual or normal

repair (ri per′) to fix or mend

rocket (räk′ it) a device that is pushed

into the air by gases that are released
from the rear

satellite (sat′ ə līt) a planet, moon, or
object made by people that moves
around a larger object

scientist (sī′ ən tist′) a person who
studies nature and the universe

simple (sim′ pəl) easy; not difficult

soil (soil) the top layer of ground

solid (sol′ id) something that is not a
liquid or gas

space (spās) the area of the whole universe

spacecraft (spās′ kraft) a ship for
traveling in space

space shuttle (spās shut′ əl) a special
kind of spacecraft that takes off like a
rocket and lands like an airplane

space suit (spās′ soot) clothing for
living and moving in space

speed (spēd) rate of motion; how fast or
slow something is moving

spin (spin) to turn around and around. A
top spins around.

squeeze (skwēz) to press hard on the sides of something

stage (stāj) a section or part of a rocket with its own engine

strap (strap) to hold with strips of material

string (string) threads twisted into a single line

suck (suk) to draw something into the mouth

supply (sə plī′) enough of something that is needed

surface (sur′ fis) the top of something

telescope (tel′ ə skōp′) an instrument used to look at the sun, moon, stars planets, and other objects in the sky; it makes objects look bigger and closer than they actually are

temperature (tem′ pər ə chər) the amount of heat or coldness

thousand (thou′ zənd) the number 1,000

toothpaste (tooth′ pāst′) a thick paste used for cleaning teeth

transmitter (trans′ mit ər) something that sends out radio or television signals

travel (trav′ əl) to go to or move to another place

tube (to͞ob) something that holds things. A toothpaste tube is a container of soft metal or plastic that is squeezed to get the toothpaste out.

twinkle (twing′ kəl) to blink on and off quickly; to sparkle

warmth (wôrmth) the state of being warm

weightless (wāt′ ləs) having no weight or heaviness

Bibliography

Fradin, Dennis B. *Moon Flights*. Chicago: Childrens Press, 1985.

Fradin, Dennis B. *Space Colonies*. Chicago: Childrens Press, 1985.

Fradin, Dennis B. *Spacelab*. Chicago: Childrens Press, 1984.

Gaffney, Timothy R. *Kennedy Space Center*. Chicago: Childrens Press, 1985.

Greene, Carol. *Astronauts*. Chicago: Childrens Press, 1984.

Haskins, Jim. *Space Challenger*. Minneapolis: Carolrhoda Books, 1984.

Hawkes, Nigel. *Space Shuttle*. New York: Gloucester Press, 1983.

Kerrod, Robin. *Living in Space*. Windermere, Florida: Rourke, 1984.

O'Connor, Karen. *Sally Ride and The New Astronauts*. New York: Franklin Watts, 1983.

Vogt, Gregory. *A Twenty-fifth Anniversary Album of NASA*. New York: Franklin Watts, 1983.